Your Mind Matters
John R. W. Stott

**The Place of
the Mind in the
Christian Life**

**InterVarsity Press
Downers Grove
Illinois 60515**

© 1972 by Inter-Varsity Press, London.
Third American printing, October 1975
by InterVarsity Press with permission
from Universities and Colleges
Christian Fellowship, England.

InterVarsity Press is the book
publishing division of Inter-Varsity
Christian Fellowship, a student
movement active on campus at
hundreds of universities, colleges
and schools of nursing.
For information about local
and regional activities, write
IVCF, 233 Langdon St.,
Madison WI 53703.

ISBN 0-87784-441-0
Library of Congress Catalog
Card Number: 72-94672

Printed in the United
States of America

Contents

Other books by John R. W. Stott
Balanced Christianity
The Baptism and Fullness of the Holy Spirit
Basic Christianity
Basic Introduction to the New Testament
Christ the Controversialist
Christian Mission in the Modern World
Guard the Gospel
Men Made New

Booklets by John R. W. Stott
The Authority of the Bible
Becoming a Christian
Being a Christian
Divorce
Evangelism: Why and How
Personal Evangelism

Foreword

Nobody wants a cold, joyless, intellectual Christianity. But does this mean we should avoid "intellectualism" at all costs? Is it experience, rather than doctrine, that really matters? Many students close their minds with their textbooks, satisfied that the intellect should play little, if any, part in the Christian life. How far are they right? For the Christian, enlightened by the Spirit, just what is the place of the mind?

These are questions of vital practical importance; they affect all aspects of our faith. To what extent, for example, should we appeal to people's reason in our presentation of the gospel? Does "faith" imply something completely irrational? Does common sense play any part in the Christian's guidance?

It was with these and other problems in view

that the Rev. John Stott gave his Presidential Address at the 1972 Inter-Varsity Fellowship Annual Conference on the place of the mind in the Christian life. This booklet gives the full text of his address. It explains why the use of the mind is so important for the Christian and how it applies to practical aspects of the Christian life. It makes a forceful appeal to Christians to show "devotion set on fire by truth."

The Publisher

1
Mindless Christianity

What Paul wrote about unbelieving Jews in his day could be said, I fear, of some believing Christians in ours: "I bear them witness that they have a zeal for God, but it is not enlightened."[1] Many have zeal without knowledge, enthusiasm without enlightenment. In more modern jargon, they are keen but clueless.

Now I thank God for zeal. Heaven forbid that knowledge without zeal should replace zeal without knowledge! God's purpose is both, zeal directed by knowledge, knowledge fired with zeal. As I once heard Dr. John Mackay say, when he was President of Princeton Seminary, "Commitment without reflection is fanaticism in action. But reflection without commitment is the paralysis of all action."

The spirit of anti-intellectualism is prevalent

today. The modern world breeds pragmatists, whose first question about any idea is not "Is it true?" but "Does it work?" Young people tend to be activists, dedicated supporters of a cause, though without always inquiring too closely either whether their cause is a good end to pursue or whether their action is the best means by which to pursue it. An undergraduate from Melbourne, Australia, while attending a conference in Sweden, heard that a student protest had started in his own university. He wrung his hands in dismay. "I *wish* I were back home," he cried. "I'd have been in it. What's it all about?" He had zeal without knowledge.

Mordecai Richler, the Canadian commentator, has been very outspoken on this issue: "What scares me about this generation is the extent to which ignorance is their armour. If know-nothingness goes on much longer, somebody will yet emerge from a commune having discovered . . . the wheel."[2]

This same specter of anti-intellectualism rises regularly to haunt the Christian church. It regards theology with distate and distrust. Let me give you some examples.

Catholic Christians have nearly always placed a strong emphasis on ritual and its proper performance. This at least has been a traditional feature of Catholicism, even if many contemporary Catholics (influenced by the liturgical movement) prefer the simple, not to say the austere. Now outward ceremonial is not to be despised if it is a clear and seemly expression of biblical truth. The danger of ritual is that it easily degenerates into ritualism, that is, into a mere performance in which the ceremony has become an end in itself, a meaningless substitute for intelligent worship.

Radical Christians, on the other hand, are concentrating their energies on social and political action. The preoccupation of the ecumenical movement is no longer with ecumenicity itself, or with church union schemes, or with questions of faith and order, but rather with feeding the hungry, housing the homeless, combating racism, securing justice for the oppressed, promoting aid programs in developing nations and supporting the revolutionary movements of the underprivileged world. Although the issues of violence and of Christian political involvement are controversial, in general one must pronounce the struggle for the well-being, dignity and freedom of all men a Christian quest. Nevertheless, historically speaking, this new preoccupation owes much of its impetus to the widespread despair of ever reaching doctrinal agreement. Ecumenical activism thrives on the rebound from the task of theological formulation, a task which cannot be avoided if the world's churches are ever to be reformed and renewed, let alone united.

My third example is Pentecostal Christians, many of whom make experience the major criterion of truth. Leaving aside questions regarding the validity of what they seek and claim, one of the most serious features at least of some neo-Pentecostalism is its avowed anti-intellectualism. One of the movement's leaders said recently, apropos of the Catholic Pentecostals, that what matters in the end is "not doctrine but experience." This is tantamount to putting our subjective experience above the revealed truth of God. Others say they believe that God is deliberately giving people unintelligible utterance in order to bypass—and so humble—their proud intellect. Well, God certainly abases the pride of men, but he does not despise the mind which he himself has made.

These three emphases—of many Catholics on ritual, radicals on social action, and Pentecostals on experience—are all to some extent symptoms of the same malady of anti-intellectualism. They are escape routes by which to avoid our God-given responsibility to use our minds Christianly.

In negative terms I would like to subtitle this essay "the misery and menace of mindless Christianity." More positively, I want to try to summarize the place of the mind in the Christian life. Let me survey the field I hope to cover.

In the second chapter, by way of introduction, I shall marshal some arguments—both secular and Christian—why it is important for us to use our minds. In the third, as my main thesis, I shall describe six aspects of Christian life and responsibility in which the mind occupies an indispensable place. In conclusion, I shall issue some cautions against jumping out of the frying pan into the fire, that is, against abandoning a superficial anti-intellectualism in favor of an arid hyper-intellectualism. I am not pleading for a dry, humorless, academic Christianity, but for a warm devotion set on fire by truth. I long for this biblical balance and the avoidance of fanatical extremes. I shall urge that the remedy for an exaggerated view of the intellect is neither to disparage it, nor to neglect it, but to keep it in its God-appointed place, fulfilling its God-appointed role.

2
Why use
our
minds?

Why should Christians use their minds?

The first reason will appeal to every believer who longs to see the gospel spread and Jesus Christ acknowledged throughout the world. It concerns the power of men's thoughts to shape their actions. History is full of examples of the influence of great ideas. Every powerful movement has had its philosophy which has gripped the mind, fired the imagination and captured the devotion of its adherents. One has only to think of the Fascist and Communist manifestos of this century, of Hitler's *Mein Kampf* on the one hand and of Marx's *Das Kapital* and the *Thoughts* of Chairman Mao on the other. A. N. Whitehead sums it up:

The great conquerors, from Alexander to Caesar, and from Caesar to Napoleon, influenced profoundly the lives of subsequent generations. But the total effect of this influence shrinks to insignificance, if compared to the entire transformation of human habits and human mentality produced by the long line of men of thought from Thales to the present day, men individually powerless, but ultimately the rulers of the world.[1]

Much of today's world is dominated by ideologies which, if not totally false, are alien to the gospel of Christ. We may talk of "conquering" the world for Christ. But what sort of "conquest" do we mean? Not a victory by force of arms. Our Christian crusade is far different from the shameful crusades of the Middle Ages. Listen to Paul's description of the battle: "Our war is **13** not fought with weapons of flesh, yet they are strong enough, in God's cause, to demolish fortresses. We demolish sophistries, and the arrogance that tries to resist the knowledge of God; every thought is our prisoner, captured to be brought into obedience to Christ."[2] This is a battle of ideas, God's truth overthrowing the lies of men. Do we believe in the power of the truth?

Not long after Soviet Russia's brutal suppression of the Hungarian uprising in 1956, Mr. Krushchev referred to the example set by Tsar Nicholas I, whose Russian forces had repressed the Hungarian revolt of 1848. In a debate on Hungary in the General Assembly of the United Nations, Sir Leslie Munro quoted Mr. Krushchev's remarks and concluded his speech by recalling a statement made by Lord Palmerston in the House of Commons on July 21, 1849, on the same subject. This is what Palmerston had said:

Opinions are stronger than armies. Opinions, if they are founded in truth and justice, will in the end prevail against the bayonets of infantry, the fire of artillery and the charges of cavalry. . . .[3]

I turn now from secular examples of the power of thought to some more specifically Christian reasons for using our minds. My argument now is that the great doctrines of creation, revelation, redemption and judgment all imply that man has an inescapable duty both to think and to act upon what he thinks and knows.

14

created to think

I begin with creation. God made man in his own image, and one of the noblest features of the divine likeness in man is his capacity to think. It is true that all subhuman creatures have brains, some rudimentary, some more developed. Mr. W. S. Anthony of the Oxford Institute of Experimental Psychology read a paper to the British Association in September, 1957, in which he described certain experiments with rats. He put obstacles before their food and water "goal-boxes," which had frustrated them in their attempts to find their way through the maze. He discovered that, faced with the more complicated mazes, his rats showed signs of what he called "primitive intellectual doubt"! That may well be. But if some creatures have doubts, only man has what the Bible calls "understanding."[4]

Scripture assumes and portrays this from the beginning of man's creation. In Genesis 2 and 3 we see God communicating with man in a way that he does not communicate with animals. He expects man to cooperate with him, consciously and intelligently, in tilling and keeping the garden in which he has placed him, and to discriminate—rationally as well as morally—between what he is permitted to do and the one thing he is prohibited from doing. Moreover, God invites man to name the animals, symbolizing the lordship over them which he has been given; and he creates woman in such a way that man immediately recognizes her suitability as his life partner and, as a result, breaks spontaneously into the first love poem ever composed!

This basic rationality of man by creation is everywhere taken for granted. Indeed, Scripture bases upon it the regular argument that since man *is* different from the animals he should *behave* differently: "Be not like a horse or a mule, without understanding."[5] Consequently, man is mocked and rebuked both when his behavior is more bestial than human ("I was stupid and ignorant, I was like a beast toward thee"[6]) and when the behavior of animals is more human than that of some human beings. For sometimes animals actually outshine humans. Ants are more industrious and more prudent than the human sluggard. Oxen and donkeys tend to give their masters a more obedient recognition than God's people. And migratory birds are better at repentance, for when they go away on migration they always return, whereas some backsliders go and fail to come back.[7]

The theme is clear and compelling. There are many similarities between man and the animals. But animals were created to behave by instinct, human beings (*pace* the behaviorists) by intelligent choice. So when humans fail to do by their own mind and consent what animals do by instinct, they are contradicting themselves, contradicting their creation and their distinctive humanity, and they ought to be ashamed of themselves.

It is quite true that man's mind has shared in the devastating results of the Fall. The "total depravity" of man means that every constituent part of his humanness has been to some degree corrupted, including his mind, which Scripture describes as "darkened." Indeed, the more men suppress the truth of God which they know, the more "futile," even "senseless," they become in their thinking. They may claim to be wise, but they are fools. Their mind is "the mind of the flesh," the mentality of a fallen creature, and it is basically hostile to God and his law.[8]

All this is true. But the fact that man's mind is fallen is no excuse for a retreat from thought into emotion, for the emotional side of man's nature is equally fallen. Indeed, sin has more dangerous effects on our faculty of feeling than on our faculty of thinking, because our opinions are more easily checked and regulated by revealed truth than our experiences.

So then, in spite of the fallenness of man's mind, commands to *think*, to use his mind, are still addressed to him as a human being. God invites rebellious Israel: "Come now, let us reason together, says the Lord."[9] And Jesus accused the unbelieving multitudes, including the Pharisees and Sadducees, of being able to interpret the sky and forecast the weather but quite unable to interpret "the signs of the times" and forecast the judgment of God. "Why do you not judge for yourselves what is right?" he asked them. In other words, why don't you use your brains? Why don't you apply to the spiritual and moral realm the common sense which you use in the physical?[10]

What Scripture teaches concerning man's **17** basic rationality, constituted by his creation and not altogether destroyed by his fall, secular society everywhere assumes. Advertisers may address their appeal to our baser appetites, but they take for granted our ability to distinguish between products; indeed, they often try to flatter the "discriminating" customer. When a crime is first reported by the news media, it is often added that "no motive has yet been discovered." It is assumed, you see, that even criminal behavior has a motivation of some kind. And when our behavior is more emotional than rational, we still insist on "rationalizing" it. The very process called "rationalization" is significant. It indicates that man has been constituted such a rational being that if he has no reasons for his behavior he has to invent some in order to live with himself.

thinking God's thoughts

I turn now from creation to revelation. The simple and glorious facts that God is a self-revealing God and that he has revealed himself to man indicate the importance of our minds. For all God's revelation is rational revelation, both his general revelation in nature and his special revelation in Scripture and in Christ.

Take nature. "The heavens are telling the glory of God; and the firmament proclaims his handiwork. Day to day pours forth speech, and night to night declares knowledge. There is no speech, nor are there words; their voice is not heard; yet their voice goes out through all the earth, and their words to the end of the world."[11] That is to say, God speaks to man through the created universe and proclaims his divine glory, although it is a message without words. The message is quite clear, however, and men who stifle its truth are guilty before God. "For what can be known about God is plain to them, because God has shown it to them. Ever since the creation of the world his invisible nature, namely his eternal power and deity, has been clearly perceived in the things that have been made. So they are without excuse, for although they knew God they did not honor him as God. . . ."[12]

Both these passages refer to God's self-revelation through the created order. Although it is a proclamation without speech, a voice without words, yet as a result of it all men to some degree "know God." This assumed ability of man to read what God has written in the universe is extremely important. All scientific research depends upon it, upon a correspondence between the character of what is being investigated and the mind of the investigator. This correspondence is *rationality*. Man is able to comprehend the processes of nature. They are not mysterious. They are logically explicable in terms of cause and effect. Christians believe that this common rationality between man's mind and observable phenomena is due to the Creator who has expressed his mind in both. As a result, in the astronomer Kepler's famous words, men can "think God's thoughts after him."

The same essential correspondence is even more direct between the Bible and the Bible reader. For in and through Scripture God has *spoken*, that is, communicated in words. One may perhaps say that if in nature God's revelation is visualized, in Scripture it is verbalized, and in Christ it is both, for he is "the Word made flesh." Now communication in words presupposes a mind which can understand and interpret them. For words are meaningless symbols until they are deciphered by an intelligent being.

So the second Christian reason why the human mind is important is that Christianity is a revealed religion. I doubt if this point has been better expressed than by James Orr in his book *The Christian View of God and the World:*

If there is a religion in the world which exalts the office of teaching, it is safe to say that it is the religion of Jesus Christ. It has been frequently remarked that in pagan religions the doctrinal element is at a minimum—the chief thing there is the performance of a ritual. But this is precisely where Christianity distinguishes itself from other religions—it does contain doctrine. It comes to men with definite, positive teaching; it claims to be the truth; it bases religion on knowledge, though a knowledge which is only attainable under moral conditions . . . A religion divorced from earnest and lofty thought has always, down the whole history of the Church, tended to become weak, jejune and unwholesome; while **20** *the intellect, deprived of its rights within religion, has sought its satisfaction without, and developed into godless rationalism.*[13]

Some people, to be sure, have reached the opposite conclusion. Since man is finite and fallen, they argue, since he cannot discover God by his intellect and God must reveal himself, therefore the mind is unimportant. But no. The Christian doctrine of revelation, far from making the human mind unnecessary, actually makes it indispensable and assigns to it its proper place. God has revealed himself in *words* to *minds*. His revelation is a rational revelation to rational creatures. Our duty is to receive his message, to submit to it, to seek to understand it and to relate it to the world in which we live.

That God needs to take the initiative to reveal himself shows that our minds are finite and fallen; that he chooses to reveal himself to babies[14] shows that we must humble ourselves to receive his Word; that he does so at all, and in words, shows that our minds are capable of understanding it. One of the highest and noblest functions of man's mind is to listen to God's Word, and so to read his mind and think his thoughts after him, both in nature and in Scripture.

I venture to say that when we fail to use our minds and descend to the level of animals, God addresses us as he addressed Job when he found him wallowing in self-pity, folly and bitter complaining: "Gird up your loins like a man, I will question you, and you shall declare to me."[15]

minds renewed

We now move on from the doctrine of revelation to the doctrine of redemption, the redemption which God has achieved through the death and resurrection of Jesus Christ. Having achieved it through his Son, he now announces it through his servants. Indeed, the proclamation of the gospel—again addressed in words to minds—is the chief means which God has appointed to bring salvation to sinners. Paul puts it like this:

For since, in the wisdom of God, the world did not know God through wisdom, it pleased God through the folly of what we preach to save those who believe.[16]

Notice carefully the contrast which the apostle is making. It is not between a rational and an irrational presentation, as if to say that, since human wisdom could not discover God, God has dispensed with a rational message altogether. No. What Paul is contrasting with human wisdom is divine revelation. But it is a rational revelation, "what we preach," the *kerygma* of Christ crucified and risen. For, although men's minds are dark and their eyes are blind, although the unregenerate cannot by themselves receive or understand spiritual things "because they are spiritually discerned,"[17] nevertheless the gospel is still addressed to their minds, since it is the divinely ordained means of opening their eyes, enlightening their minds and saving them. I shall have more to say about this when we come to the subject of evangelism.

22 Now redemption carries with it the renewal of the divine image in man, which was distorted by the Fall. This includes the mind. Paul could describe converts from paganism as having "put on the new nature, which is being renewed in knowledge after the image of its creator"[18] and as "being renewed in the spirit of your minds."[19] He could go further. A "spiritual" man, a man indwelt and ruled by the Holy Spirit, has new powers of spiritual discernment. He may even be said to have "the mind of Christ."[20]

This conviction that Christians have new minds enabled Paul to appeal to his readers with confidence: "I speak as to sensible men; judge for yourselves what I say."[21]

I find myself wondering how the apostle would react if he were to visit Western Christendom today. I think he would deplore, as Harry Blamires has justly deplored, the contemporary lack of a Christian mind. A "Christian mind" is described by Mr. Blamires as "a mind trained, informed, equipped to handle data of secular controversy within a framework of reference which is constructed of Christian presuppositions,"[22] presuppositions (for example) of the supernatural, of the pervasiveness of evil, of truth, authority and the value of the human person. The Christian thinker, he goes on, "challenges current prejudices . . . disturbs the complacent . . .obstructs the busy pragmatists . . . questions the very foundations of all about him and . . . is a nuisance."[23] But, he says, Christian thinkers with Christian minds do not seem to exist today. On the contrary:

The Christian mind has succumbed to the secular drift with a degree of weakness and nervelessness unmatched in Christian history. It is difficult to do justice in words to the complete loss of intellectual morale in the twentieth-century Church. One cannot characterize it without having recourse to language which will sound hysterical and melodramatic. There is no longer a Christian mind. There is still, of course, a Christian ethic, a Christian practice, and a Christian spirituality. . . . But as a thinking *being, the modern Christian has succumbed to secularization.*[24]

It is a sad denial of our redemption by Christ, whom God is said to have "made our wisdom."[25]

judged by our knowledge

The fourth Christian doctrine which presupposes the importance of the mind is the doctrine of judgment. For if one thing is clear about biblical teaching on the judgment of God, it is that he will judge us by our knowledge, by our response (or lack of response) to his revelation.

Take as an Old Testament example the book of Jeremiah. Jeremiah predicted by the word of the Lord, with great personal courage and unremitting persistence, that unless the people listened to God's voice their nation, city and temple would be destroyed. But instead of listening, they shut their ears, stiffened their necks and hardened their hearts. These are some of the key phrases of the book. Here are a few examples:

From the day that your fathers came out of the land of Egypt to this day, I have persistently sent all my servants the prophets to them, day after day; yet they did not listen to me, or incline their ear, but stiffened their neck.[26]

... I brought them [your fathers] out of the land of Egypt ... saying, Listen to my voice, and do all that I command you. So shall you be my people, and I will be your God. ... I solemnly warned your fathers when I brought them up out of the land of Egypt, warning them persistently, even to this day, saying, Obey my voice. Yet they did not obey or incline their ear, but everyone walked in the stubbornness of his evil heart.[27]

For twenty-three years ... the word of the

Lord has come to me, and I have spoken persistently to you, but you have not listened. You have neither listened nor inclined your ears to hear, although the Lord persistently sent to you all his servants the prophets. . . .[28]

They have turned to me their back and not their face; and though I have taught them persistently they have not listened to receive instruction.[29]

Even after Jerusalem had been destroyed by Nebuchadnezzar and the hapless Jeremiah had himself been reluctantly carried off to Egypt, he continued to warn his Jewish compatriots of the judgment of God on the wickedness of his people:

I persistently sent to you all my servants the prophets, saying, "Oh, do not do this abominable thing that I hate!" But they did not listen or incline their ear. . . .[30]

This principle of judgment our Lord himself endorsed:

He who rejects me and does not receive my sayings has a judge; the word that I have spoken will be his judge on the last day.[31]

And the essence of the argument of the apostle Paul in the early chapters of his letter to the Romans is that all men are guilty before God precisely because all men possess some knowledge—the Jews through God's written law and the Gentiles through nature and through God's law written on their hearts—but no man has lived up to the knowledge he has.

It is a solemn thought that by our anti-intellectualism, in which we either refuse or cannot be bothered to listen to God's word, we may be storing up for ourselves the judgment of Almighty God.

I have tried to show how basic is man's rationality to the great doctrines of creation, revelation, redemption and judgment. God has constituted us thinking beings; he has treated us as such by communicating with us in words; he has renewed us in Christ and given us the mind of Christ; and he will hold us responsible for the knowledge we have.

Perhaps the current mood (cultivated in some Christian groups) of anti-intellectualism begins now to be seen as the serious evil it is. It is not true piety at all but part of the fashion of the world and therefore a form of worldliness. To denigrate the mind is to undermine foundational Christian doctrines. Has God created us rational beings, and shall we deny our humanity which he has given us? Has God spoken to us, and shall we not listen to his words? Has God renewed our mind through Christ, and shall we not think with it? Is God going to judge us by his Word, and shall we not be wise and build our house upon this rock?[32]

It is not surprising, in view of these doctrines, to discover how much emphasis Scripture—in both Old and New Testaments—places upon the acquisition of knowledge and wisdom. In the Old Testament God complained that his people behaved like "stupid children" who had "no understanding"[33] and declared that they were "destroyed for lack of knowledge."[34] All the wisdom literature of the Old Testament was given them to stress that only "fools hate knowledge" and that only the wise man is truly happy since in gaining wisdom he has something "better than gold" and "more precious than jewels."[35]

Similarly in the New Testament much of the apostles' instruction is directed to the acquisition of divine wisdom and its application to holy living. "Make every effort," wrote Peter, "to supplement your faith with virtue, and virtue with knowledge. . . ."[36] "Among the mature we do impart wisdom," wrote Paul, and went on to chide the Corinthians for their immaturity. They were still like babies, he said, needing milk and unable to digest the solid food of heavenly wisdom.[37]

So Paul's great prayers for the young churches and their members were all first and foremost that they might grow in knowledge and that the Holy Spirit might exercise his ministry among and within them as the Spirit of truth.

For the Ephesians he prayed "that the God of our Lord Jesus Christ, the Father of glory, may give you a spirit of *wisdom* and revelation in the *knowledge* of him, having the eyes of your hearts enlightened, that you may *know* what is the hope to which he has called you, what are the riches of his glorious inheritance in the saints, and what is the immeasurable greatness of his power in us who believe. . . ."[38]

Later in the same letter he prayed that they

might "be strengthened with might through his Spirit in the inner man, and that Christ may dwell in your hearts through faith." Why? Here was the reason: "that you, being rooted and grounded in love, may have power to *comprehend* with all the saints what is the breadth and length and height and depth, and to *know* the love of Christ which surpasses *knowledge*, that you may be filled with all the fulness of God."[39]

For the Philippians he prayed "that your love may abound more and more, with *knowledge* and all *discernment*, so that you may approve what is excellent, and may be pure and blameless for the day of Christ, filled with the fruits of righteousness. . . ."[40]

For the Colossians he prayed "that you may be filled with the *knowledge* of his will in all spiritual *wisdom* and *understanding,* to lead a life worthy of the Lord, fully pleasing to him, bearing fruit in every good work and increasing in the *knowledge* of God."[41]

The repetition of these words *knowledge, wisdom, discernment* and *understanding* is surely very striking. There can be no doubt that the apostle regarded these as the very foundation of the Christian life.

3
The mind in the Christian life

We are now in a position to consider in what ways God expects us to use our minds. It is not my purpose here to defend the acquisition of "secular" knowledge or "culture," but rather to outline six spheres of Christian living, each of which is impossible without the proper use of the mind. We shall examine in turn Christian worship, Christian faith, Christian holiness, Christian guidance, Christian evangelism and Christian ministry.

true worship

I am rather fond of the story (and have quoted it in *Christ the Controversialist*[1]) which used to be told by an American minister, the late Dr. Rufus M. Jones. He believed in the important place of the intellect in preaching. But one of his congregation objected to his emphasis and wrote to him to complain. "Whenever I go to church," said his critic, "I feel like unscrewing my head and placing it under the seat, because in a religious meeting I never have any use for anything above my collar button!"

Such mindless worship was certainly offered in pagan Athens where Paul found an altar dedicated "to an unknown god."[2] But it is not becoming in Christians. The apostle was not content to leave the Athenians in their ignorance. He proceeded to proclaim to them the nature and works of the God they ignorantly worshipped. For he knew that the only worship acceptable to God is intelligent worship, worship "in truth," the worship offered by those who know whom they are worshipping and who love him "with all their mind."[3]

The Psalter was the great hymnbook of the Old Testament church, and the Psalms are still sung in Christian worship today. It is instructive, therefore, to learn from this source what true worship is. The basic definition of worship in the Psalter is to "praise the name of the Lord," or to "ascribe to the Lord the glory due to his name."[4] And when we begin to inquire what is meant by his "name," we find that it is the sum total of all that he is and has done. In particular, he is worshipped in the Psalms as both the Creator of the world and the Redeemer of Israel, and the Psalmists delight in their praises to give lengthy catalogs of God's works of creation and redemption.

Psalm 104, for example, expresses open-eyed wonder at the wisdom of Gods manifold works, in the sky and the earth, in animal and vegetable life, among birds and mammals and the "things innumerable" with which the great and wide sea teems.

Psalm 105, on the other hand, celebrates a different set of God's "wonderful works," namely his special dealings with his covenant people. It rehearses the history of the centuries, God's promises to Abraham, Isaac and Jacob, his providence toward Joseph in Egypt exalting him from prison to princedom, his mighty acts through Moses and Aaron, sending the plagues and rescuing the people, his provision for them in the wilderness and his power in causing them to inherit the promised land. Psalm 106 tells much the same story but marvels this time at God's patience with his people, who kept forgetting his works, disbelieving his promises and rebelling against his commands.

Psalm 107 praises God for his steadfast love in redeeming different groups of people from their particular plight, travellers lost in the desert, prisoners languishing in a dungeon, the sick who draw near to death and seafarers caught in a mighty storm. These all "cried to the Lord in their trouble, and he delivered them from their distress." So "let them thank the Lord for his steadfast love, for his wonderful works to the sons of men!"

My last example is Psalm 136. Here the same liturgical refrain occurs in every verse: "for his steadfast love endures for ever." And the summons to give thanks to the Lord for his goodness begins with his creation of the heavens, the earth, the sun, the moon and the stars, and then goes on to his redemption of Israel from Egypt and from the Amorite kings, in order to give them their land as a heritage.

These examples are enough to show that Israel did not worship God as some distant or abstract deity but as the Lord of nature and of nations, one who had revealed himself in concrete acts, by creating and sustaining his world, and by redeeming and preserving his people. They had good cause to praise him for his goodness, for his works and for "all his benefits."[5]

To these mighty deeds of God (the creation-God and the covenant-God), Christians add the mightiest deed of all in the birth, life, death and exaltation of Jesus, his gift of the Spirit and his new creation, the church. Such is the story of the New Testament, and this is why readings from the Old and the New Testament together with a Scripture exposition are an indispensable part of public worship today. Only as we hear again what God has done are we ready to respond in praise and worship. This too is why Bible reading and meditation are an essential part of a Christian's private devotion. All Christian worship, public and private, should be an intelligent response to God's self-revelation in his words and works recorded in Scripture.

It is in this context that a passing reference may be made to "speaking in tongues." Whatever glossolalia may have been in New Testament days, whether a gift of foreign languages or of ecstatic utterance, the speech was certainly unintelligible to the speaker. And this is why Paul forbade its exercise in public if there was no one to translate or interpret, and discouraged its exercise in private if the speaker continued not to understand what he was saying. He wrote: "Therefore, he who speaks in a tongue should pray for the power to interpret. For if I pray in a tongue, my spirit prays but my mind is unfruitful. What am I to do? I will pray with the spirit and I will pray with the mind also. . . ."[6] In other words, Paul could not contemplate any prayer or worship in which the mind was barren or inactive. He insisted that in all true worship the mind must be fully and fruitfully engaged. The Corinthians' cult of unintelligibility was a childish thing. They should indeed be as childish and innocent as possible in evil, but, he added, "in thinking be mature."[7]

Christian worship will not be perfected until heaven, for not until then shall we know God as he is and therefore be able to praise him as he deserves.

faith: illogical belief in the improbable?

One wonders if there is any Christian quality more misunderstood than faith. Let me begin with two negatives.

First, faith is not credulity. H. L. Mencken, the American anti-supernaturalist critic of Christianity, once said that "faith may be defined briefly as an illogical belief in the occurrence of the improbable." But Mencken was wrong. Faith is not credulity. To be credulous is to be gullible, to be entirely uncritical, undiscerning and even unreasonable in one's beliefs. But it is a great mistake to suppose that faith and reason are incompatible. Faith and sight are set in opposition to each other in Scripture,[8] but not faith and reason. On the contrary, true faith is essentially reasonable because it trusts in the character and the promises of God. A believing Christian is one whose mind reflects and rests on these certitudes.

Secondly, faith is not optimism. This seems to be the confusion made by Norman Vincent Peale. Much of what he writes is true. His fundamental conviction concerns the power of the human mind. He quotes William James that "the greatest discovery of my generation is that human beings can alter their lives by altering their attitudes of mind,"[9] and Ralph Waldo Emerson that "a man is what he thinks about all day long."[10] So Dr. Peale develops his thesis about positive thinking, which he goes on (mistakenly) to equate with faith. What exactly is the "faith" which he is advocating? His first chapter in *The Power of Positive Thinking* is significantly entitled "Believe in Yourself." In chapter 7 ("Expect the Best and Get It") he offers a suggestion which he guarantees will work. Read the New Testament, he says, collect "a dozen of the strongest statements about faith" and memorize them. "Let these faith concepts drop into your conscious mind. Say them over and over again. . . ." Gradually they will sink into your subconscious and "change you into a believer." So far this sounds promising. But wait a moment. When the Bible refers to "the shield of faith," he goes on, it is teaching a "spiritual-power technique," namely "faith, belief, positive thinking, faith in God, faith in other people, faith in yourself, faith in life. This is the essence of the technique that it teaches."[11] Dr. Peale continues by quoting splendid verses like "if thou canst believe, all things are possible to him that believeth,"[12] "if ye have faith . . . nothing shall be impossible unto you"[13] and "according to your faith be it unto you,"[14] but then he spoils it all by expounding this last text as follows: "According to your faith in yourself, according to your faith in your job, according to your faith in God this far will you get and no farther."[15]

These quotations are enough to show that Dr. Peale apparently draws no distinction between faith in God and faith in oneself. Indeed, he does not seem to be at all concerned about faith's object. He recommends as part of his "worry-breaking formula" that first thing every morning before we get up we should say out loud "I believe" three times,[16] but he does not tell us in *what* we are so confidently and repeatedly to affirm our belief. The last words of his book are simply "so believe and live successfully."[17] But believe *what*? Believe *whom*? To Dr. Peale faith is really another word for self-confidence, for a largely ungrounded optimism. I am told that Dr. Peale may have modified his position since he wrote this book, but the book is still in circulation and being read. And in that book it seems clear that his positive thinking is in the end merely a synonym for wishful thinking.

The same is true of Mr. W. Clement Stone, the philanthropist and founder of "Positive Mental Attitudes," who claims that "President Nixon would have been a soured, second-rate ex-politician if he had not thrown off his emotional immaturity by discovering PMA." "We make supermen out of ordinary men," he says, for he has developed "the sales technique to end all sales techniques." Why, "you can even sell yourself to yourself by chanting as do his salesmen every morning 'I feel happy, I feel healthy, I feel terrific!' "[18]

But neither Peale's "positive thinking" nor Stone's "positive mental attitudes" is the same thing as Christian faith. Faith is not optimism.

Faith is a reasoning trust, a trust which reckons thoughtfully and confidently upon the trustworthiness of God. For example, when David and his men returned to Ziklag, before the Philistines had killed Saul in battle, a terrible sight awaited them. During their absence the Amalekites had raided their village, burned down their houses and carried off their women and children. David and his men wept "until they had no more strength to weep," and then in their bitterness the people talked of stoning David. It was a major crisis, and David might easily have given way to despair. Instead, we read that "David strengthened himself in the Lord his God."[19] This was true faith. He did not shut his eyes to the facts. Nor did he try to build up his own self-confidence or tell himself that he was really feeling fine. No. He remembered the Lord his God, the God of creation, the God of the covenant, the God who had promised to be his God and to set him on the throne of Israel. And as David recalled the promises and the faithfulness of God, he grew strong in faith. He "strengthened himself in the Lord his God."

Thus faith and thought belong together, and believing is impossible without thinking.

Dr. Lloyd-Jones has given us an excellent New Testament example of this truth while commenting on Matthew 6:30 in his *Studies in the Sermon on the Mount:* "But if God so clothes the grass of the field, which today is alive and tomorrow is thrown into the oven, will he not much more clothe you, O men of little faith?"

Faith according to our Lord's teaching in this paragraph, is primarily thinking; and the whole trouble with a man of little faith is that he does not think. He allows circumstances to bludgeon him. . . . We must spend more time in studying our Lord's lessons in observation and deduction. The Bible is full of logic, and we must never think of faith as something purely mystical. We do not just sit down in an armchair and expect marvellous things to happen to us. That is not Christian faith. Christian faith is essentially thinking. Look at the birds, think about them, and draw your deductions. Look at the grass, look at the lilies of the field, consider them. . . . Faith, if you like, can be defined like this: It is a man insisting upon thinking when everything seems determined to bludgeon and knock him down in an intellectual sense. The trouble with the person of little faith is that, instead of controlling his own thought, his thought is being controlled by something else, and, as we put it, he goes round and round in circles. That is the essence of worry. . . . That is not thought; that is the absence of thought, a failure to think.[20]

Before leaving the place of the mind in Christian faith, I would like just to mention the two **38** ordinances, or sacraments, of the gospel, baptism and the Lord's Supper. For both are meaningful signs which are intended to bring blessing to the Christian by arousing his faith in the truths which they signify. Take the Lord's Supper. At its simplest it is a visible dramatization of the Savior's death for sinners. It is a rational reminder of it. Our minds need to play upon its meaning and grasp the assurance which it offers. Christ himself speaks to us through the bread and the wine. "I died for you," he says, and as we receive his word it should set our guilty hearts at rest again.

Thus Cranmer writes that the Lord's Supper "was ordained for this purpose, that every man, eating and drinking thereof, should remember that Christ died for him, and so should exercise his faith, and comfort himself by the remembrance of Christ's benefits. . . ."[21]

Christian assurance is the "full assurance of faith."[22] And if assurance is the child of faith, faith is the child of knowledge, the sure knowledge of Christ and of the gospel. As Bishop J. C. Ryle put it: "Half our doubts and fears arise from dim perceptions of the real nature of Christ's Gospel. . . . The root of a happy religion is clear, distinct, well-defined knowledge of Jesus Christ."[23]

the quest for holiness

Many secrets of holiness are given us in the pages of the Bible. Indeed, a major purpose of Scripture is to show God's people how to lead a life that is worthy of him and pleasing to him. But one of the most neglected aspects of the quest for holiness is the place of the mind, even though Jesus himself put the matter beyond question when he promised "you will know the truth, and the truth will make you free."[24] It is by his truth that Christ liberates us from the bondage of sin. How is this? Wherein lies the liberating power of the truth?

To begin with, we need to have a clear picture of the kind of person God intends us to be. We must know God's moral law and commandments. As John Owen expressed it, "That good which the mind cannot discover, the will cannot choose, nor the affections cleave unto." Therefore, "in Scripture the deceit of the mind is commonly laid down as the principle of all sin."[25]

The best example of this may be found in the earthly life of our Savior. Three times the devil came to him and enticed him in the wilderness of Judea. Three times he recognized that the devil's suggestion was evil and contrary to the will of God. Three times he countered the temptation with the word *gegraptai,* "it stands written." There was no room for debate or argument. The matter was settled in his mind at the outset. For Scripture had laid down what was right. This clear biblical knowledge of God's will is the first secret of a righteous life.

It is not enough to *know* what we should be, however. We must go further and set our minds upon it. The battle is nearly always won in the mind. It is by the renewal of our mind that our character and behavior become transformed.[26] So Scripture calls us again and again to mental discipline in this respect. "Whatever is true," it says, "whatever is honorable, whatever is just, whatever is pure, whatever is lovely, whatever is gracious, if there is any excellence, if there is anything worthy of praise, think about these things."[27]

Again, "If . . . you have been raised with Christ, seek the things that are above, where Christ is, seated at the right hand of God. Set your minds on things that are above, not on things that are on earth. For you have died, and your life is hid with Christ in God."[28]

Yet again, "those who live according to the flesh set their minds on the things of the flesh, but those who live according to the Spirit set their minds on the things of the Spirit. To set the mind on the flesh is death, but to set the mind on the Spirit is life and peace."[29]

Self-control is primarily mind-control. What we sow in our minds we reap in our actions. "Feed the Minds" is the slogan of a current campaign for the spread of Christian literature. It bears witness to the fact that men's minds need to be fed just as much as their bodies. And the kind of food our minds devour will determine the kind of person we become. Healthy minds have a healthy appetite. We must satisfy them with health-giving food and not with dangerous intellectual drugs and poisons.

There is, however, a second kind of mental discipline to which we are summoned in the New Testament. We are to consider not only what we should be but what by God's grace we already are. We are constantly to recall what God has done for us and say to ourselves: "God has united me with Christ in his death and resurrection, and thus obliterated my old life and given me an entirely new life in Christ. He has adopted me into his family and made me his child. He has put his Holy Spirit within me and so made my body his temple. He has also made me his heir and promised me an eternal destiny with him in heaven. This is what he has done for me and in me. This is what I am in Christ."

Paul keeps urging us to call these things to mind. "I want you to know," he writes. "I don't want you to be ignorant." And some ten times in his letters to the Romans and Corinthians he utters his incredulous question, "Don't you know?" Don't you know that by being baptized into Christ you were baptized into his death? Don't you know that you are the slaves of the one to whom you have yielded yourselves in obedience? Don't you know that you are God's temple, and that God's Spirit dwells in you? Don't you know that the unrighteous will not inherit God's kingdom? Don't you know that your bodies are members of Christ?[30]

The apostle's intention in this battery of questions is not just to make us feel ashamed of our ignorance. It is rather to prevail upon us to recall these great truths about ourselves, which in fact we know very well, and to talk to ourselves about them until their truth grips our mind and molds our character. This is not the self-confident optimism of Norman Vincent Peale. Peale's way is to get us to pretend we are other than we are. Paul's way is to remind us what we truly are, because God has made us that way in Christ.

the christian's guidance

That God is willing and able to guide his people is a fact. We know this from Scripture, from its promises (for example, Prov. 3:6, "he will make straight your paths"), from its commands (for example, Eph. 5:17, "do not be foolish, but understand what the will of the Lord is") and from its prayers (for example, Col. 4:12, "that you may stand mature and fully assured in all the will of God").

But *how* do we discover the will of God? Some Christians claim rather glibly "the Lord told me to do this" or "the Lord called me to do that," as if they had a hot line to heaven and were in direct and continuous telephonic communication with God. I find it hard to believe them. Others think they get detailed guidance from God through the most fanciful interpretations of Scripture passages which murder the natural sense, violate the context and have no basis in either sound exegesis or common sense.

If we are to discern God's will for us, we should begin by drawing an important distinction between his "general" will and his "particular" will. The "general" will of God may be so called because it is his will for all his people in general at all times, whereas the "particular" will of God may be so called because it is his will for particular people at particular times. God's general will for us is that we become conformed to the image of his Son. God's particular will, on the other hand, concerns such questions as the choice of a life work and a life partner, and the use of our time, our money and our vacations.

Once this distinction has been made, we are in a position to repeat and answer our question about how we may discover God's will. For God's general will has been revealed in Scripture. Not that it is always easy to discern his will in complex modern ethical situations. We need to have sound principles of biblical interpretation. We need to study, to discuss and to pray. Nevertheless, it remains true, regarding God's general will, that the will of God for the people of God is in the Word of God.

God's particular will, on the other hand, is not to be sought in Scripture, for Scripture does not contradict itself, and it is of the essence of God's particular will that it may be different for different members of his family. Certainly we shall find in Scripture some general principles to guide us in our particular choices. And I do not deny that some of God's people down the ages have claimed to receive very detailed guidance from Scripture. Yet I must repeat that this is not God's usual way.

Take, as an example, the question of a man and his marriage. (The illustration is, of course, equally applicable to a girl.) Scripture will guide you in general terms. It can tell you that marriage is God's good purpose for mankind, and that a single life is the exception, not the rule; that one of the primary purposes of marriage is companionship and that this is one of the qualities to look for in the girl you hope to marry; that as a Christian man you are at liberty to marry only a Christian girl; and that marriage (the full and permanent commitment of one man to one woman) is the God-ordained context in which sexual love and union are to be enjoyed. These and other vital truths about God's general will regarding marriage Scripture will tell you. But Scripture will not tell you whether your wife is to be Jane or June or Joan or Janet!

How then are you to decide this major question? There is only one possible answer, namely by using the mind and the common sense which God has given you. Certainly you will pray for God's guidance. And if you are wise, you will ask the advice of your parents and of other mature people who know you well. But ultimately you must make up your mind, trusting that God will guide you through your own mental processes.

There is good scriptural warrant for this use of the mind in Psalm 32:8-9. These two verses need to be read together and supply a fine example of the balance of the Bible. Verse 8 contains a pledge of divine guidance: "I will instruct you and teach you the way you should go; I will counsel you with my eye upon you." It is, in fact, a threefold promise: "I will instruct you, I will teach you, I will guide you." But verse 9 immediately adds: "Be not like a horse or a mule, without understanding, which must be curbed with bit and bridle, else it will not keep with you." In other words, although God promises to guide us, we must not expect him to do so in the way in which we guide horses and mules. He will not use a bit and bridle with us. For we are not horses or mules; we are human beings. We have understanding, which horses and mules have not. It is, then, through the use of our own understanding, enlightened by Scripture and prayer and the counsel of friends, that God will lead us into a knowledge of his particular will for us.

It is urgent to heed this warning of Scripture. I have known several young Christians make serious and foolish mistakes through acting on some irrational impulse or "hunch," instead of using their God-given mind. Many could echo the confession of Bernard Baruch: "Whatever failures I have known, whatever errors I have committed, whatever follies I have witnessed in private and public life have been the consequence of action without thought."[31]

presenting the gospel

In Romans 10 Paul argues cogently for the necessity of preaching the gospel if people are to become Christians. Sinners are saved, he says, by calling on the name of the Lord Jesus. That much is clear. But how can men call on someone in whom they have no faith? And how can they have faith in someone of whom they have never heard? And how can they hear of him unless a preacher tells them? He concludes his argument: "So faith comes from what is heard, and what is heard comes by the preaching of Christ."[32]

His argument implies that there must be a solid content in our evangelistic proclamation of Christ. It is our responsibility to set Jesus Christ forth in the fullness of his divine-human person and saving work so that through this "preaching of Christ" God may arouse faith in the hearer. Such evangelistic preaching is far removed from its tragic caricature, all too common today, namely an emotional, anti-intellectual appeal for "decisions" when the hearers have but the haziest notion what they are to decide about or why.

Let me invite you to consider the place of the mind in evangelism, and let me supply two reasons from the New Testament for a thoughtful proclamation of the gospel.

The first is taken from the example of the apostles. Paul summed up his own evangelistic ministry in the simple words "we persuade men."[33] Now "persuading" is an intellectual exercise. To "persuade" is to marshal arguments in order to prevail on people to change their mind about something. And what Paul claims to do Luke illustrates in the pages of the Acts. He tells us, for example, that for three weeks in the synagogue at Thessalonica Paul "argued with them from the scriptures, explaining and proving that it was necessary for the Christ to suffer and to rise from the dead, and saying, 'This Jesus, whom I proclaim to you, is the Christ.' " As a result, Luke adds, "some of them were persuaded."[34] Now all the verbs Luke uses here of Paul's evangelistic ministry—to argue, to explain, to prove, to proclaim and to persuade—are to some extent "intellectual" words. They indicate that Paul was teaching a body of doctrine and arguing towards a conclusion. He was seeking to convince in order to convert. And the fact that after a mission we tend to say "thank God some were converted" is a mark of our departure from New Testament vocabulary. It would be equally if not more biblical to say "thank God some were persuaded." At least that is what Luke said after Paul's mission in Thessalonica.

It is the reasoned nature of Paul's evangelism

which explains the long periods in which he stayed in some cities, notably Ephesus. His first three months were spent in the synagogue where he "spoke boldly, arguing and pleading about the kingdom of God." Later he withdrew from the synagogue and "argued daily in the hall of Tyrannus," which was presumably a secular lecture hall which he hired for the purpose. Some manuscripts add that his lectures went on "from the fifth hour to the tenth," that is, from eleven o'clock in the morning to four o'clock in the afternoon. And "this continued," Luke tells us, "for two years." If we may assume that he worked a six-day week, his daily five-hour lecturing for a period of two years amounts to

some 3,120 hours of gospel argument. It is not altogether surprising that, in consequence, Luke says, "all the residents of Asia heard the word of the Lord."[35] For Ephesus was the capital city of the province of Asia. Nearly everybody would come up to the city at some time, to do some shopping, or to consult a doctor, a lawyer or a politician, or to visit a relative. And evidently one of the sights of town was to go and listen to this Christian lecturer Paul. You could hear him on any day. Many did so, were persuaded of the truth of his message and went back to their villages reborn. So the word of God spread throughout the province.

The second New Testament evidence that our evangelism should be a reasoned presentation of the gospel is that conversion is not infrequently described in terms of a person's response not to

Christ himself but to "the truth." Becoming a Christian is "believing the truth," "obeying the truth," "acknowledging the truth." Paul even describes his Roman readers as having "become obedient from the heart to the standard of teaching to which you were committed."[36] It is plain from these expressions that in preaching Christ the early Christian evangelists were teaching a body of doctrine about Christ.

Let me now attempt to defend my thesis about evangelism against some objections.

First, it is sometimes asked, does not such a reasoned evangelism as I am advocating minister to people's intellectual pride? Certainly it may. We must be on our guard against this danger. At the same time there is a substantial difference **49** between flattering a person's intellectual conceit (which we must not do) and respecting his intellectual integrity (which we must do).

Secondly, does not a reasoned evangelism disqualify uneducated people from hearing the gospel? No, it does not. Or at least it should not. Like Paul we are under obligation, or in debt, "both to the wise and to the foolish."[37] The gospel is for everybody, whatever their education or lack of it. And the kind of evangelism for which I am pleading, which sets Jesus Christ forth in his fullness, is relevant to all kinds of people, children as well as adults, the uncultured as well as the cultured, Australian aboriginals as well as Western intellectuals. For the presentation implied by this evangelism is not academic —couched in philosophical terms and complicated vocabulary—but rational. And the uneducated are just as rational as the educated. Their minds may not have been trained to think in a particular way, and we should certainly take note of the distinction which Marshall McLuhan and his followers are making between linear and nonlinear thought. But they still think. All human beings think, because God made a human being a thinking creature. The teaching of Jesus himself, although beautifully simple, certainly made his listeners think. He presented them with great truths about God and man, about himself and the kingdom, about this life and the next. And he often ended his parables with a teasing question to force his hearers to make up their minds on the issue under discussion.

50

Our duty then is to avoid distorting or diluting the gospel, and at the same time to make it plain, to cut the word of truth straight so that people can follow it,[38] lest "when any one hears the word of the kingdom *and does not understand it,* the evil one comes and snatches away what is sown in his heart."[39] I fear that our clumsy explanations sometimes give the devil this very opportunity which he ought never to be allowed.

Thirdly, does not a reasoned evangelism usurp the work of the Holy Spirit and thus effectively dispense with it? Now of course there can be no evangelism without the power of the Holy Spirit. But it is a grave mistake to suppose that to give doctrinal content to the good news and to use arguments to demonstrate its truth and relevance is a mark of either self-confidence or unbelief, and that if only we had more faith in the Holy Spirit we could omit all doctrine and arguments. The opposite is, in fact, the case. To set the Holy Spirit and a reasoned presentation of the gospel over against each other is a false antithesis.

What Paul had renounced, he told the Corinthians, was the wisdom of the world (as the substance of his message) and the rhetoric of the Greeks (as his method of presenting it). Instead of worldly wisdom he resolved to preach Christ and him crucified, and instead of rhetoric to rely on the power of the Spirit. But he still used doctrine and arguments.

Gresham Machen expressed this matter admirably in his book *The Christian Faith in the Modern World*: "There must be the mysterious work of the Spirit of God in the new birth," he wrote. "Without that, all our arguments are quite useless. But because argument is insufficient, it does not follow that it is unnecessary. What the Holy Spirit does in the new birth is not to make a man a Christian regardless of the evidence, but on the contrary to clear away the mists from his eyes and enable him to attend to the evidence."[40]

Wolfhart Pannenberg, the young Professor of Systematic Theology at Munich, has written something similar in his *Basic Questions in Theology*: "An otherwise unconvincing message cannot attain the power to convince simply by appealing to the Holy Spirit. . . . Argumentation and the operation of the Spirit are not in competition with each other. In trusting in the Spirit Paul in no way spared himself thinking and arguing."[41]

So then in our evangelistic proclamation we must address the whole person (mind, heart and will) with the whole gospel (Christ incarnate, crucified, risen, reigning, coming again, and much else besides). We shall argue with his mind and plead with his heart in order to move his will, and we shall put our trust in the Holy Spirit throughout. We have no liberty to present a partial Christ (man but not God, his life but not his death, his cross but not his resurrection, the Savior but not the Lord). Nor have we any liberty to ask for a partial response (mind but not heart, heart but not mind, or either without the will). No. Our objective is to win a total man for a total Christ, and this will require the full consent of his mind and heart and will.

I pray earnestly that God will raise up today a new generation of Christian apologists or Christian communicators, who will combine an absolute loyalty to the biblical gospel and an unwavering confidence in the power of the Spirit with a deep and sensitive understanding of the contemporary alternatives to the gospel; who will relate the one to the other with freshness, pungency, authority and relevance; and who will use *their* minds to reach *other* minds for Christ.

the ministry and its gifts
My sixth and last example of the place of the mind is Christian ministry. We have to use our

mind in every kind of ministry, but especially in the ordained or pastoral ministry of the church.

There is a good deal of renewed interest today in the subject of ministry and in the *charismata* (gifts of the Spirit) which qualify and equip God's people for their ministry. All spiritual gifts (and there are many) are intended for ministry of some kind. They are given to be exercised "for the common good,"[42] their purpose being to build up the church, the body of Christ, that it may grow up into maturity. The gifts most to be coveted and prized, therefore, are the *teaching* gifts, since it is by these that the church is most "edified" or built up.

Such a teaching gift is certainly necessary for presbyters, who have the pastoral care of the local church. We shall take a look both at the nature of their ministry and at the necessary qualifications for it.

The "ordained" ministry is essentially a "pastoral" ministry, and a "pastoral" ministry is a "teaching" ministry. Let me elaborate this. The minister is a pastor, a shepherd, entrusted by Christ the chief shepherd with the care of a part of his flock and charged in particular to feed (that is, teach) them.

Thus the apostle Paul could say to the presbyter-bishops of the Ephesian church: "Take heed to yourselves and to all the flock, in which the Holy Spirit has made you guardians [overseers], to feed the church of the Lord which he obtained with his own blood."[43]

And the apostle Peter, who had himself three

times been commissioned by the risen Lord to tend or feed his sheep and lambs,[44] wrote later to other presbyters: "Tend the flock of God that is your charge. . . ."[45]

Dropping the pastoral metaphor, the ultimate responsibility of local presbyters is to "present every man mature in Christ." And for the attainment of this goal they must proclaim Christ in his fullness, "warning every man and teaching every man in all wisdom."[46] It is by the knowledge of Christ as he is portrayed in the Scriptures and proclaimed by the ministry that Christians reach spiritual maturity.

The qualifications for the ministry are consistent with its nature. Every candidate for the pastoral ministry or the presbyterate must possess both the biblical faith and a gift for teaching it. He must be orthodox. "He must hold firm to the sure word as taught [literally 'according to the *didache*,' or the apostles' teaching], so that he may be able to give instruction in sound doctrine and also to confute those who contradict it."[47] He must also be "an apt teacher." [48] These are two of his indispensable qualifications. He must be loyal to the *didache* and he must be *didaktikos*, a teacher of the teaching.

This will involve him in study, both in his preparation for the ministry and in his exercise of it. It is very striking that those who wish to commend themselves in every way as God's ministers must do so, Paul wrote, not only by their patient endurance of hardship, nor only by their purity, forbearance, kindness and love, but also by their *knowledge*.[49]

I was thankful to hear Dr. Billy Graham say, when addressing some 600 ministers in London in November, 1970, that if he had his ministry all over again he would study three times as much as he had done. "I've preached too much and studied too little," he said. The following day he told me of Dr. Donald Barnhouse's statement: "If I only had three years to serve the Lord, I would spend two of them studying and preparing."

I myself have a growing burden that God will call out more men for this teaching ministry today; that he will call men with alert minds, biblical convictions and an aptitude for teaching; that he will set them in the great capital cities and university cities of the world; that there, like Paul in Tyrannus's hall in Ephesus, they will exercise a thoughtful, systematic teaching ministry, expounding the ancient Scriptures and relating them to the modern world; and that such a faithful ministry under the good hand of God will not only lead their own congregation up to Christian maturity but will also through the visitors who come briefly under its influence spread its blessing far and wide.

4
Acting on our knowledge

At the beginning of this booklet, I mentioned the risk of jumping out of the frying pan into the fire, that is, the peril of overreaction, of turning from a barren anti-intellectualism to an equally barren hyper-intellectualism. We shall easily avoid this danger if we remember just one thing: God never intends knowledge to be an end in itself but always to be a means to some other end.

I have tried to sketch six spheres of Christian living in which the mind plays an essential part —Christian worship, faith, holiness, guidance, evangelism and ministry. If these things are impossible without using our minds and acquiring some biblical knowledge, we must also recognize the corollary, that the acquisition of biblical knowledge must lead into these things and enrich our experience of them. Knowledge carries with it the solemn responsibility to act on the knowledge we have, to translate our knowledge into appropriate behavior. Let me enlarge on this.

First, knowledge should lead to worship. The true knowledge of God will result not in our being puffed up with conceit at how knowledgeable we are, but in our falling on our faces before God in sheer wonder and crying, "O the depth of the riches and wisdom and knowledge of God! How unsearchable are his judgments and how unscrutable his ways!"[1] Whenever our knowledge becomes dry or leaves us cold, something has gone wrong. For whenever Christ opens the Scriptures to us and we learn from him, our heart should be aglow within us.[2] The more we know God the more we should love him. I believe it was Bishop Handley Moule who said that we should beware equally of an undevotional theology and an untheological devotion.

Secondly, knowledge should lead to faith. We have already seen that knowledge is the foundation of faith and makes faith reasonable. "Those who know thy name put their trust in thee," wrote the psalmist.[3] It is our very knowledge of God's nature and character which elicits our faith. But if we cannot believe without knowing, we must not know without believing. That is, our faith must grasp hold of whatever truth God reveals to us. Indeed, God's message brings no benefit unless it meets with faith in the hearers.[4]

This is why Paul does more than pray that the eyes of our hearts may be enlightened to *know* the greatness of God's power which has been demonstrated in the resurrection; he adds that this power which God accomplished in Christ is now available to us who *believe*. The first and necessary step is that we know in our minds the magnitude of God's power, but this should lead us to appropriate his power in our lives by faith.[5]

Thirdly, knowledge should lead to holiness. We have considered some ways in which our conduct could be transformed if only we knew more clearly both what we should be and what we already are. But now we have to see how the more our knowledge grows, the greater our responsibility is to put it into practice. Many biblical examples could be quoted. Psalm 119 is full of aspirations to *know* God's law. Why? In order the better to *obey* it: "Give me understanding, that I may keep thy law and observe it with my whole heart."[6] The Lord Jesus said to the twelve: "If you know these things, blessed are you if you do them."[7] Paul wrote: "What you have learned and received and heard and seen in me, do."[8] And James was emphasizing the same principle when he urged his readers to be "doers of the word, and not hearers only" and warned them that faith without works was but a dead orthodoxy shared with demons.[9]

Thomas Manton, the Puritan minister, who at one time was Oliver Cromwell's chaplain, likened a disobedient Christian to a child suffering from rickets: "Rickets cause great heads and weak feet. We are not only to dispute of the word, and talk of it, but to keep it. We must neither be all ear, nor all head, nor all tongue, but the feet must be exercised!"[10]

Fourthly, knowledge should lead to love. The more we know, the more we should want to share what we know with others and use our knowledge in their service, whether in evangelism or in ministry. Sometimes, however, our love will restrain our knowledge. For by itself knowledge can be harsh; it needs the sensitivity which love can give it. This is what Paul meant when he wrote: "Knowledge puffs up, but love builds up."[11] The "man of knowledge" he was talking about is the instructed Christian who knows that God is one, that idols are nothing and that there is therefore no theological reason why he may not eat food which has previously been offered to idols. There may be a practical reason for refraining, however. For some Christians do not possess this knowledge, and as a result their conscience is "weak," that is, uninstructed and overscrupulous. They were themselves previously idolaters. And even after their conversion they find they cannot with a good conscience eat idol-meats. In their company, therefore, Paul argues, the "strong" or instructed Christian should abstain in order not to offend his "weak" brother's conscience. He himself has liberty of conscience to eat. But his love will limit the liberty which his knowledge gives him. Perhaps it is against this kind of background that a few chapters later Paul goes so far as to say: "If I . . . understand all mysteries and all knowledge . . . but have not love, I am nothing."[12]

Let us heed these warnings. Knowledge is indispensable to Christian life and service. If we do not use the mind which God has given us, we condemn ourselves to spiritual superficiality and cut ourselves off from many of the riches of God's grace. At the same time, knowledge is given us to be used, to lead us to higher worship, greater faith, deeper holiness, better service. What we need is not less knowledge but more knowledge, so long as we act upon it.

If you ask how such knowledge is to be attained, I cannot do better than reply in some words of one of Charles Simeon's sermons: "For the attainment of divine knowledge we are directed to combine a dependence on God's Spirit with our own researches. Let us, then, not presume to separate what God has thus united."[13] That is to say, we must pray and we must study. This is what Daniel was told: "Fear not, Daniel, for from the first day that you set your mind to understand and humbled yourself before your God, your words have been heard. . . ."[14] Indeed, both the setting of the mind to understand and the self-humbling before God are tokens of a man's hunger for divine truth. Such hunger will surely be satisfied. For God has promised that the earnest seeker will find:

My son, if you receive my words and treasure up my commandments with you, making your ear attentive to wisdom and inclining your heart to understanding; yes, if you cry out for insight and raise your voice for understanding, if you seek it like silver and search for it as for hidden treasures; then you will understand the fear of the Lord and find the knowledge of God. For the Lord gives wisdom; from his mouth come knowledge and understanding. [15]

Notes

Chapter 1
1/Romans 10:2.
2/From Mordecai Richler's review of Richard Neville's *Play Power* (New York: Random House, 1970) in the *Guardian Weekly* on February 28, 1970.

Chapter 2
1/Quoted by H. J. Blackham in *Humanism* (Harmondsworth: Penguin, 1968), p. 101.
2/2 Corinthians 10:4-5, Jerusalem Bible.
3/Quoted by *The Times* (London) UN correspondent in New York on December 8, 1959.
4/Psalm 32:9.
5/Ibid.
6/Psalm 73:22.
7/Proverbs 6:6-11; Isaiah 1:3; Jeremiah 8:7.
8/Ephesians 4:18; Romans 1:18-23; 8:5-8.
9/Isaiah 1:18.
10/Matthew 16:1-4; Luke 12:54-57.
11/Psalm 19:1-4.
12/Romans 1:18-21.
13/James Orr, *The Christian View of God and the World* (Grand Rapids: Eerdmans, 1954), pp. 20-21. First published in 1893.
14/Matthew 11:25.
15/Job 38:3; 40:7.
16/1 Corinthians 1:21.
17/1 Corinthians 2:14; 2 Corinthians 4:3-6.
18/Colossians 3:10.
19/Ephesians 4:23. The Greek should, I believe, be translated as an indicative, not an imperative.
20/1 Corinthians 2:15-16.
21/1 Corinthians 10:15.
22/Harry Blamires, *The Christian Mind* (London: SPCK, 1963), p. 43.
23/Ibid., p. 50.
24/Ibid., p. 3.
25/1 Corinthians 1:30.
26/Jeremiah 7:25-26.
27/Jeremiah 11:4, 7-8.
28/Jeremiah 25:3-4.
29/Jeremiah 32:33.
30/Jeremiah 44:4-5.
31/John 12:48.
32/Cf. Matthew 7:24-27.
33/Jeremiah 4:22. Compare the phrase in Proverbs 30:2, "I am too stupid to be a man."
34/Hosea 4:6; cf. Isaiah 5:13.
35/Proverbs 1:22; 3:13-15.
36/2 Peter 1:5.
37/1 Corinthians 2:6; 3:1-2; cf. Hebrews 5:11—6:3.
38/Ephesians 1:17-19.
39/Ephesians 3:14-19.

40/Philippians 1:9-11.
41/Colossians 1:9-10.

Chapter 3
1/John R. W. Stott, *Christ the Controversialist* (Downers Grove, Ill.: Inter-Varsity Press, 1970).
2/Acts 17:23.
3/John 4:24; Luke 10:27.
4/Psalms 148:5, 13; 96:8; 115:1.
5/Psalm 103:2.
6/1 Corinthians 14:13-15.
7/1 Corinthians 14:20.
8/2 Corinthians 5:7.
9/Norman Vincent Peale, *The Power of Positive Thinking* (Tadworth: World's Work, 1953), p. 220.
10/Ibid., p. 223.
11/Ibid., pp. 118-19.
12/Mark 9:23.
13/Matthew 17:21.
14/Matthew 9:29.
15/Peale, p. 126.
16/Ibid., p. 169.
17/Ibid., p. 302.
18/From an interview with Adam Raphael reported in the *Guardian Weekly*, March 20, 1971.
19/1 Samuel 30:1-6.
20/D. Martyn Lloyd-Jones, *Studies in the Sermon on the Mount* (Grand Rapids: Eerdmans, 1960), II, 129-30.
21/Thomas Cranmer, *On the Lord's Supper* (Parker Society edition, 1844), p. 352.
22/Hebrews 10:22.
23/J. C. Ryle, *Expository Thoughts on the Gospels* (Grand Rapids: Zondervan, 1955), IV, 321, 80.

24/John 8:32.
25/John Owen, *Pneumatologia* or *A Discourse Concerning the Holy Spirit* (1668), p. 111.
26/Romans 12:2.
27/Philippians 4:8.
28/Colossians 3:1-2.
29/Romans 8:5-6.
30/Romans 6:3, 16; 1 Corinthians 3:16; 6:9, 15; cf. also 1 Corinthians 5:6; 6:2-3, 16, 19.
31/Quoted by Ted. W. Engstrom and Alec Mackenzie in *Managing Your Time* (Grand Rapids: Zondervan, 1967), p. 120.
32/Romans 10:13-14, 17.
33/2 Corinthians 5:11.
34/Acts 17:2-4.
35/Acts 19:8-10.
36/Romans 6:17.
37/Romans 1:14.
38/Cf. 2 Timothy 2:15.
39/Matthew 13:19.
40/J. Gresham Machen, *The Christian Faith in the Modern World* (Grand Rapids: Eerdmans, 1947), p. 63. First published in 1936.
41/Wolfhart Pannenberg, *Basic Questions in Theology* (London: SCM, 1971), II, 34-35.
42/1 Corinthians 12:7; cf. 1 Peter 4:10-11.
43/Acts 20:28.
44/John 21:15-17.
45/1 Peter 5:2.
46/Colossians 1:28.
47/Titus 1:9; cf. 1 Timothy 4:13; 2 Timothy 2:15.
48/*Didaktikos;* 1 Timothy 3:2; cf. 2 Timothy 2:24.
49/2 Corinthians 6:6.

Chapter 4

1/Romans 11:33.
2/Cf. Luke 24:32.
3/Psalm 9:10.
4/Cf. Hebrews 4:2.
5/Ephesians 1:18-20.
6/Psalm 119:34.
7/John 13:17.
8/Philippians 4:9.
9/James 1:22-25; 2:14-26.
10/Thomas Manton, *An Exposition of John 17,* a comment on verse 6 (Sovereign Grace Book Club, 1958), p. 117.
11/1 Corinthians 8:1.
12/1 Corinthians 13:2.
13/The conclusion of his Sermon no. 975.
14/Daniel 10:12.
15/Proverbs 2:1-6.